Now What?

The LifeWay, Way of Living...

By

Pastor Stephen Cianci

& Pastor Joel Rissinger

All rights reserved. No part of this publication may be reproduced or transmitted for commercial purposes, except for brief quotations in printed reviews, without written permission of the author.

Unless otherwise indicated, Scripture taken from the New King James Version. Copyright © 1982 by Thomas Nelson, Inc. Used by permission. All rights reserved.

Dedication

To our wives Tina and Karen plus our staff, our Executive Leadership Team, our Board of Stewardship and our fantastic ministry leaders at LifeWay Church: This book is your heart and ours. Thank you for all you do!

Table of Contents

Introduction: Why This Book?   Page 5

Chapter

    1. Baptism & Communion   Page 6
    2. Finding a Life-Giving Church.   Page 13
    3. The Steps to Freedom in Christ   Page 19
    4. Finding a Mentor in your Life Group. Page 21
    5. 7 Habits of Highly Effective Believers: Page 27
        a. Fellowship & Life Groups,
        b. Prayer,
        c. Bible Study,
        d. Service,
        e. Giving,
        f. Faith-Sharing, and
        g. Mentoring others.

Conclusion…   Page 56

Footnotes…   Page 57

Appendix…   Page 58

        Statement of Faith…

        Bridge Diagram…

        "5 in 5" & "7 in 7" Cards…

Introduction

If you've been around LifeWay Church for more than a minute, you've no doubt heard us say, "We exist to reach the one." We want to reach the one who may be isolated, hurting, confused, etc.; and help them connect to God, connect to others of faith, and then to connect to people in the community at large.

This book is a critical part of that effort. In fact, it really deals with all three components of that vision: God, other believers, and the community around us. We hope you'll find it helpful in those efforts.

You're reading this because you've decided to make a faith commitment to Jesus Christ as Lord and Savior. As the title of this book asks, "Now What?" These first steps will guide as you grow in your faith and help others do the same.

To that end,

Pastors Steve & Joel

Chapter One:

Baptism and Communion...

Your First Acts of Faith

Scripture tells us that when Jesus went to John the Baptist and sought to be baptized, John resisted. After all, if anyone didn't need baptism it was Jesus. Furthermore, John felt Jesus should baptize HIM, not the other way around.

Who wouldn't feel this way?

What's interesting is Jesus' answer to John. He said, "Let it be so now; it is proper for us to do this to fulfill all righteousness." Then John consented (Matthew 3:15, NIV). In other words, Jesus is saying, I need to obey just like everyone else. Actually, He would say he needed to fulfill and obey everything the Father commanded such that He'd be a perfect sacrifice, the only fully obedient human in history! And praise God, He was!

The point here is that Jesus saw baptism as an act of obedience and faith. So should we. Some say, "Well, I was baptized as an infant so why do it again?" Others say, "Well I'm saved by faith, not works so why do I need to be baptized?" Then, there are the various methods of baptism: sprinkling, pouring, immersion, triple immersion, etc. People want to know which to use and whether or not it matters.

Let's try to tackle these in order. First, infant baptism. There is a key difference between a believer's baptism as a teen or and adult versus the baptism or christening of an infant. The difference is regarding the source of the faith being demonstrated by the baptism. Baptism is an act of obedience, as Jesus demonstrated, but it's an obedience based on faith. So whose faith is involved? With an infant, it's clearly the parent's faith since the child has no idea what's happening. To be a personal act of faith and obedience, the person must be old enough to come to faith and want to express it. This is why our church and most other evangelical churches, practice a believer's baptism and not a baptism for infants. We wouldn't consider it a "second baptism" if the person had been christened as a baby. In fact, we'd consider it a first, since it would be the first time the individual was expressing their personal faith in this way.

As to the second question, if we're saved by faith, why do we need baptism; I'd go further and ask this: if you're saved by faith, why do anything God asks you to do? Couldn't you just live your life the way you want and forget about any acts of obedience? Shoot, let's make it fun—why not sin on purpose to demonstrate God's mercy? Paul asked this rhetorically in Romans 6:1. His answer, "God forbid (Verse 2)!" The answer is simple, if you committed to following Jesus wherever He might lead, the first act of obedience was the same as his act at age 30, to be baptized as an outward demonstration of inner faith.

Regarding methods, the answer is also quite simple. Multiple verses refer to baptisms taking place where was "much water," (John 3:23, etc.). Jesus is said to have come up "out of the water" after his baptism as did others in Scripture (Mark 1:10, etc.). In fact the Greek word used in the New Testament for baptize literally means to "dip under," or "immerse." Furthermore, the symbolism of baptism is death and rebirth—or newness of life. Thus, it's helpful to realize that when a person dies, we don't just pour a little dirt on their head and leave them lying on the floor or the middle of the street. Rather, we bury them. Thus immersion seems to be the natural and logical choice.

Having said this, I want to be clear that baptism doesn't save us and immersion is not commanded in the Bible. We know it was the common practice of the early church, but the method is not as important at the meaning. Thus, here at LifeWay, if I had someone who physically couldn't be immersed or was terrified of water, I'd sprinkle them. I would point out that in 25 years of ministry, I've never had to sprinkle or pour and I've baptized hundreds of people. Still, I know in principle, it's the meaning, not the method that matters.

Once someone expresses Biblical faith in Jesus, they should be baptized right away. In Acts 2, the 3,000 believers were baptized that same day. That may not be possible or necessary, but waiting for months is unwise because it appears rebellious and may open the person to spiritual attack from the Enemy, Satan the Devil, who sees the delay as an opening or lack of faith.

Briefly, we should also mention that when we baptize people at LifeWay, we pray over them asking for another baptism, or the complete filling of the Holy Spirit. We believe that this blessing is available to all believers and it results in the granting of and initiation of spiritual gifts. We discuss this more during our Growth Track series of classes, but suffice it to say that we believe all believers have access to the full power of the Holy Spirit and we ask for it when they are water baptized as well as at other times as appropriate.

Timing is also an issue regarding the Lord's Supper/Communion. Since Communion pictures the Lord's death and that taking in and embracing Christ's sacrifice via symbols of his body and blood, doing it before we're saved is silly. In fact, it can be dangerous as well. Paul warned the Corinthian Christians against taking it lightly saying that some had even died due to their cavalier and sinful attitudes towards the Lord's Table. They were known for getting drunk on the wine and overeating, often selfishly gobbling up the bread and other items before others got to share. God was greatly displeased with this and the Enemy apparently took advantage of it (See I Cor. 11:17-34).

I've always said that taking communion or being baptized before you accept Christ would be like having a wedding anniversary while you're still engaged. You can't celebrate what happened before it happened. That wouldn't make sense.

But what about the elements and the frequency of communion? Should we use leavened or unleavened bread? Juice or wine? Should we do it weekly, daily, monthly, annually?

Truthfully, the Bible doesn't prescribe or dictate these details. We know the first Lord's Supper was conducted at Passover so Jesus no doubt used unleavened bread and wine. We also know that, while Jesus never commanded it, the early church took it both in weekly public meetings and "from house to house," presumably during the week (Acts

2:41-47). Still, we're not commanded to repeat this practice per se.

What we CAN gather as timeless principles are that we should do it fairly often as a means of remembering what Jesus has done for us. We can also gather that bread and grape juice or wine are the best symbols of His body and blood. We can also say that it isn't necessary for a priest or ministry to administer the symbols since there's no way even the early church practiced this with 3,000 people meeting in homes during the week and only 12 apostles to "go around."

So a new Christian should fellowship with a church and both be baptized and take Communion regularly. As to what church they should attend, and what else should happen in the new believer's journey, that's what we'll cover next.

Chapter Two:
Finding a Life-Giving Church

Of course we'd love to have you become a member of LifeWay Church! Still, for others you may work with or if you have to transfer to another city someday, we trust this chapter will be helpful.

The Bible promotes a very high view of the Church. It's Jesus' bride (Rev. 19 & Eph 5:31-32), his "Body, (I Cor 12:27)," "the pillar and foundation of the truth (I Tim. 3:15)," and more! Despite her problems, the church deserves our respect, commitment and service.

How?

Well, first let's deal with the common misconception that being a good Christian is a solo act. It's true that no man is an island. This is even more applicable to church involvement. Pastor Rick Warren tells a story of a man who said, "Rick, I'm an independent Christian, I'm part of the invisible church." Rick's response was, "Oh, I see. So when you're in the hospital, does the invisible pastor come to see you and the invisible deacons mow your lawn? Do you serve the invisible widows and donate to the invisible building fund?"

You get the idea.

While it's true that spiritual new birth brings each of us into the universal family or church, it's also true that we need a nuclear or local family where we belong and serve as a committed member. This is no different than the human experience. As a human baby, I was born into the greater human family. Still, I depended on and am committed to my nuclear family (Mom, Dad and Sister) more than I am to people I've never met in outer-Mongolia, etc.

But where and how do I find that local church body?

In most of the world, the diversity of the Body of Christ is both a blessing and a curse. The blessing is that there are multiple styles, formats, and priorities to choose from. Literally, there's "something for everyone," when it comes to choosing a church home. The bad news is that the choice has driven a certain consumer mentality where we liken choosing a church to choosing a store or a favorite restaurant to hang-out in when we have a night on the town.

Local churches are a part of the larger Body and shouldn't be treated like our favorite supermarket. Our involvement is MUCH more important than being a "frequent shopper." Jesus said, "Give and it will be given to you…(Luke 6:38)." So our choice of churches should be based more on what we can contribute than on what we think we'll "get" in return.

I say this with a couple of caveats. First, I'm assuming that the churches you're considering teach the truth. That is, they hold to the essentials of the Christian faith (see our Statement of Faith in the appendix). I would argue there about 12 major doctrines or beliefs that all Christians hold to and many other peripheral things on which we may differ. For the sake of this discussion, let's assume you're looking at 3-4 churches all of whom subscribe to those 12 primary beliefs.

Second, I'm assuming that the church has biblical leadership. What I mean is that the pastor and other senior leaders are living lives in sync with I Timothy chapter 3 and Titus chapter one and are qualified to lead. In other words, none are abusive or living an openly sinful lifestyle which would disqualify them from leadership.

If these things are in place, then the choice really becomes one of calling. The only question that matters is, "Where is God calling me to serve?" He may call you to serve in a small, new, church plant where the building isn't as nice. He may call you to a place that has an inferior kids program, lower quality music, or maybe even a pastor that doesn't preach like Billy Graham. Why would you choose THAT church over the sexy megachurch across town with the laser light shows and the cool pastor who rides a motorcycle up on stage each week before preaching the proverbial house down?!!

Because you feel a call to serve.

In the long run, people who actively feel needed and are serving, using their gifts and talents, grow more spiritually and find greater satisfaction than do the "consumer Christians" who choose a church based on personal desire versus God's calling. That's just a fact.

To assist you should you choose to make LifeWay Church your home, we offer three things:

1. Our Dream Team. A host of ministries you can choose from to find a place to serve and connect.
2. LifeWay Cares Ministry. A group of ministries focused on reaching out to our community to do servant evangelism—sharing the gospel by meeting needs and sharing our testimonies.
3. Our "Growth Track." Growth Track consists of 4 different classes or seminars to help you understand the church (101), connect with God (201), connect with others in ministry by finding yours and getting involved (301), and by connecting with the

community at large both locally and globally (401). To find out more about these, contact any of our staff or volunteer leaders.

So pray. Seek council from other believers and leaders. Look for needs that you can fill with the attributes God has given you. Then choose a church, commit to membership, serve, and grow like crazy!

Chapter Three:

The Steps to Freedom in Christ

Everyone has hurts, habits, and hang-ups. Many struggle with negative thoughts, lustful thoughts, angry outbursts, addictions, relationship problems, and more.

The good news is that Jesus has made a way to be free from these things. The bad news is that many Christians don't take advantage of that opportunity. In the book of James in the New Testament, James tells us that if we submit and draw close to God, He'll draw close to us. He also says that if we resist the Devil, he will flee (See James 4:7-8). We believe this is critical to walk in the fullness of blessing God offers.

At LifeWay Church, we use a tool to help people overcome the strongholds in their life. It's called, "The Steps to Freedom in Christ" and it was originally produced by Dr. Neil Anderson.

"The Steps to Freedom in Christ" is a 7-part prayer process. We start with a confidential review of your life where you ask God to help you see where different spiritual strongholds may have been established. Then, with a prayer partner and an encourager, you pray through 7 areas of life where these strongholds often exist. Jesus, the true Freedom-giver, will bless you in this process by breaking loose the chains of hurts and hang-ups. It is a wonderful, truth-encounter time with God that at the least, will leave you feeling peaceful and, at best, may lead to miraculous results in your life.

While not mandatory, we recommend that every new Christian set up a Freedom Appointment with a member of our Freedom Ministry Team members. They will help you find out more about the Steps. They'll also recommend that your read two of Neil's books, *"Victory Over Darkness,"* and *"The Bondage Breaker"* to help you both understand this ministry as well as to prepare to go through the "Steps to Freedom," should you choose to do so. You can contact our Freedom Ministry Team at 860-436-9216,

Chapter Four:
Finding a Mentor in Your Life Group

Perhaps the greatest missing dimension in modern Christian discipleship strategy is mentoring. Churches typically offer wonderful large group worship experiences, attractive small group ministry opportunities, and great Bible Studies or Sunday School Classes. But sadly, millions of believers participate in all that for years and yet experience a life virtually unchanged as compared to what they lived prior to trusting in Christ. We joke that some people have 30 years of Christian experience while many others have one year they've repeated 30 times.

Why?

George Barna and others have written on this and provide some wonderful data worthy of analysis. They've shown us the sad reality that when it comes to divorce, child abuse, drug abuse, bankruptcy, and other sad experiences of life—the percentage of Christians guilty of these is no different than non-Christians. I'd recommend you read my book, "The Crucified Church," for more information on this and some suggestions of how to change it.[3]

I'm sure there are many reasons for this and all of the influencing factors need to be explored. Still, I believe the one thing we haven't done which might have significantly decreased the number of believers in each of these categories, is to provide one-on-one or one-on-two or at the most, three, mentoring.

I can hide in a church of 30,000. So could you. I know of people who have attended megachurches for 10 years or more and are still asked weekly, "Is this your first time here?" But you don't have to attend a megachurch to hide. I've seen people hide in a small group of 10-15 people. If they're shy, they may come in, say "Hi," and sit quietly the whole night and be virtually invisible. But try as we might, it is IMPOSSIBLE to hide in a one-on-one meeting over coffee.

Mentoring allows for individual attention. It allows each person to be loved and taught or encouraged based on their unique personality, motivation, spiritual giftedness, life experience, etc. No other venue offers that kind of powerful focus. But the good news is, anyone seeking it can find it!

At our church, we sponsor and encourage mentoring. We have people in leadership whose job it is to help find mentors for new or existing believers. These leaders host what we call, "Life Groups," groups of 5-12 who meet to grow, support, encourage, and serve together. Within those groups, it is our hope that you'll find someone to meet with one-on-one or at most, one-on-two-or-three to study God's Word, pray, etc. If you haven't already joined one, this would be the first step toward finding a good spiritual mentor. You can find a list of Life Groups at www.lifewaych.com.

When you meet, we have to simple tools to assist, "5 in 5" and "7 in 7" where two or three people meet for either 5 or 7 weeks to study the Bible and talk. Each week has a theme or topic with a few verses written on a 3'x5" card (see appendix). Still, the focus is individual needs and attention. The goal at the end of 7 in 7 is for the mentee to become the mentor and find someone else to engage with through this process.

Pastors, deacons, ministry leaders, new believers—all need and benefit from being mentored and from mentoring. So how do you find the right person to mentor you so you can in turn "teach others" (II Timothy 2:1-2)?

Here are some tips:

1. Find someone who's a step or two ahead of you in their spiritual journey. You won't learn much from an agnostic if you're a new believer. Obviously, a mature Christian has more to offer you at this stage. This is true throughout your life—there will always be people you can look up to and learn from.

2. Find someone who has some things in common with you. This will allow the two of you to connect or relate better and thus grow faster.

3. With rare exception, find someone the same gender as you. Mentoring shouldn't be romantic and unless your mentor is your spouse, attraction could at least slow your growth if not become a potentially bigger problem.

4. Find someone in your Life Group, or if not, at least from our church. This is simply for convenience and to be sure you're on the "same page" as the leaders of your church and the direction or focus God has given them, etc.

5. If you have trouble locating someone, talk with your Life Group leader, pastor, elders, or other leaders to see who they'd recommend.

Before closing this chapter, let me (Pastor Joel) say a word about coaching. I believe there is a distinction between a coach and a mentor. A mentor teaches and encourages—sometimes even challenges or lovingly corrects us. A coach, on the other hand, is someone who asks us questions and listens to help us discover what God is saying and what we may already know inside at a subconscious level. I think the best case scenario is to find both a coach and a mentor. Still, since coaching is an art and something that requires some training and skill, a mentor alone would be a great step forward.

Chapter Five:

The Seven Habits of Highly Effective Believers

Sadly, Christianity has become complicated. There are more than 450,000 churches in the U.S. alone and none of them are exactly alike. Oh sure, there are denominational groupings with similar doctrines, but even so, individual churches within those denominations have their own distinct style, focus, and personality.

I should clarify that I don't think that's entirely bad. Diversity and uniqueness are part of how God creates. Just looking at nature, we can see that. In addition, different styles of worship reach different kinds of people who might not come to know Jesus otherwise. I'm all for that!

The sad part isn't the variety and distinctiveness, it's the legalistic importance we give to things that aren't emphasized in scripture. Quite frankly, the reason for the kaleidoscope of Christianity is the fact that we're often divided over minor, even silly issues.

Churches have split over the name of the church, music preferences, even the composition of the bread at communion. The sad thing is that most of these positions, pro or con, aren't supported by scripture nor can any precedent be found in early church history. Still, people "divide and conquer," based on these and other non-essentials.

I once pastored in a Baptist church where the 118 year old tradition was having communion bread made from an old Swedish recipe. When it became apparent that the deaconesses who made the bread couldn't keep up the demand for more and more loaves each month, we switched to matzos. At the time, I explained that unleavened bread was most likely what Jesus used to institute the Lord's Supper anyway and most were satisfied. Some, on the other hand, were enraged! One lady even stopped eating the bread we passed around during communion. Instead, she'd bring her own bread from home in a little baggie and when the plate was passed, she'd reach into her purse and take "the real bread," instead of what the rest of us were sharing.

True story!

So when it comes to walking the Christian walk, what really matters? What SHOULD we focus on? Jesus said the disciples were to "teach (converts) to obey all things I have commanded... (Matt. 28:20)." Thus, it seems logical to focus on the things Jesus and the Apostles focused on. We might have other traditions and practices which are fine and even helpful. Still, most of our time—especially when new to the faith—should be spent mastering what I call the "Magnificent 7" of Christian living:

1. Fellowship,
2. Prayer,
3. Bible Study,
4. Service,
5. Giving,
6. Faith-Sharing, and,
7. Mentoring others.

Now knowing our tendency to "major in the minors" and quibble over little things, I need to justify my list. I know the knee-jerk reaction some will have is, "Yes, but what about _____ (insert favorite pet dogma here)?" Others will say, "OK, but where did Jesus address _____ (pick any on my list)?"

Dr. Stephen Covey had his "7 Habits of Highly Effective People," and I've borrowed the idea for the title of this chapter because I believe scripture focuses on these 7 disciplines as the way Christians grow in their walk. So before exploring these 7 in detail, let's establish a biblical foundation for choosing them specifically, no more and no less.

First, let's consider what's often called the Great Commandment and the Great Commission of Matthew 22 and 28:

> *Matt. 22:35 Then one of them, a lawyer, asked Him a question, testing Him, and saying, [36] "Teacher, which is the great commandment in the law?" [37] Jesus said to him, "'You shall love the LORD your God with all your heart, with all your soul, and with*

all your mind.³⁸ This is the first and great commandment. ³⁹ And the second is like it: 'You shall love your neighbor as yourself.' ⁴⁰ On these two commandments hang all the Law and the Prophets."

Matt. 28:19 Go therefore and make disciples of all the nations, baptizing them in the name of the Father and of the Son and of the Holy Spirit, ²⁰ teaching them to observe all things that I have commanded you; and lo, I am with you always, even to the end of the age." Amen.

From these two passages of scripture, we see several of the "Magnificent 7." From the greatest commandment, loving God, we are led to connect with Him regarding prayer and time listening to Him through His Word, the Bible. If we look at the second great commandment, loving others, and from Matthew 28, we see sharing our faith and mentoring others. By extension, we see fellowship—spending time and connecting with other people of faith. If we love as we love ourselves, clearly we'd also give and serve—offering our money and time to help them.

So, just from these two passages, we've found biblical support for all 7 items of focus. Still, let's look at "day one" of the early church, immediately after it was launched on Pentecost, circa 33 A.D:

> *Acts 2:41 Then those who gladly received his word were baptized; and that day about three thousand souls were added to them. [42] And they continued steadfastly in the apostles' doctrine and fellowship, in the breaking of bread, and in prayers. [43] Then fear came upon every soul, and many wonders and signs were done through the apostles. [44] Now all who believed were together, and had all things in common, [45] and sold their possessions and goods, and divided them among all, as anyone had need.[46] So continuing daily with one accord in the temple, and breaking bread from house to house, they ate their food with gladness and simplicity of heart, [47] praising God and having favor with all the people. And the Lord added to the church daily those who were being saved.*

This time, we see almost all of the "Magnificent 7" in one passage and, an indication of the foundational value of these 7 over many other practices of the modern Church.

They valued the Bible (Apostles teaching), fellowship (including regular communion), prayer, giving, serving (by sacrifice), sharing faith with others. Actually, the only item not explicitly mentioned is mentoring, but we can assume its existence based on both the fruit of this early churches' ministry and the context.

So having explored the biblical foundation for the 7 Habits, let's take a closer look at each one and how we can apply it to everyday life…

Fellowship

I love to joke that if you have two fellows in the same boat, you've got a "fellow-ship." As corny as that sounds, there's some truth to it. As believers, we ARE in the same boat and can help each other through some of life's challenges. This is why we spent so much time talking about finding a good church in Part I of this book. The Bible commands us not to avoid spending time together—especially as the time for Jesus' second coming draws near (Heb. 10:25).

The problem in the U.S. and in much of the developed western world is that we are too independent. We claim to be rugged individualists who need no one and "stand on our own two feet." We don't want spiritual relationships for fear that someone might try to tell us what to do. This mindset is wrong and leaves us vulnerable like a sheep wandering away from the flock. The Bible is full of references to the need for a unified Body that learns, grows, and is safer together (Eph. 4, I Cor 12, I Peter 5:8, etc.).

Fellowship becomes that basis for so much growth in the life of a believer. It's what church gatherings can be. It is thus a foundation for corporate worship and prayer. It's where mentors and mentees are found. It's what we invite seekers into before they become fellow-believers. Fellowship is also the essence of how communion is shared as one body and where the celebration of baptism becomes so special and powerful. Loner or extravert, we need fellowship.

Many churches, as we do at LifeWay, encourage small group or Life Group ministry participation. The reason, among other things, is fellowship. We know we need each other and the easiest way to make deep connections is in a small group setting. We love Life Groups because we literally "do life" together. Sure, there's power and fellowship in a large church service. But beyond a quick, "How-ya doin?," most of us don't go too deep on Sunday mornings. If you haven't tried it, visit a small group soon and see the difference. To find out about the Life Groups available at LifeWay, go to http://lifewaych.com/life-groups/.

Prayer

Prayer is nothing more, or less, than a conversation with God. Too often, we worry about having, "just the right words" in order to pray. We even memorize formal prayers for church and other occasions, yet we fail to think through the whole relational essence of prayer.

I recently asked my church to consider how it would feel if someone they loved read a pre-written comment from a 3x5" card every time they met. That's bad enough, but imagine it was the SAME message every time. "Hello _____, I like and appreciate you. Please continue to be my friend. I'm hoping you'll have a wonderful day. Thank you for everything. Love, Me."

How would you feel?

Horrible right? So how is it that we assume God loves hearing the "Our Father," or the "Rosary" or the same canned "Grace" prayer over meals again, and again, and again…and again? Especially when we repeat it in a boring, monotone voice! It sometimes is slurred or repeated so quickly that it comes-off sounding like Charlie Brown's teacher in the old Peanuts cartoons. "Blaaa, bla, blaaa, blaa, blaaaaaaa!"

No, real prayer is simply sharing what's on your mind with God either out loud or silently, but intentionally. It also involves times of silence where we "listen" to see if God gives us a prompting via a thought or an image to inspire more prayer/conversation. Many times, reading the Bible during these sessions prompts a sense of God's direction and love. Sometimes, it inspires even more comment from us.

Another helpful tool for approaching prayer is to use some of the "canned" prayers we know as a springboard for more conversation. For example, I believe Jesus gave us the "Lord's Prayer/Our Father," as an outline or teaching tool for prayer. It gives us the components of a healthy prayer time. Here's what I mean:

Phrase	**Prayer Topic**
"Our Father…Hallowed be Thy Name."	Worship/Praise
"Thy Kingdom Come"	The Church
"Give Us This Day…."	Provision
"Forgive us…as we forgive"	Confession
"Lead us not into temptation"	Avoiding sin.
"Thine is the kingdom and the power…"	Praise/Worship

I like to think of this outline as a "praise sandwich" because it opens and closes with praise like two slices of bread. However you view it, PLEASE don't view it like a magic incantation we repeat over and over until God gives us what we want. It's an outline for conversation—prayer—with Almighty God.

Praying out loud with others is another powerful tool many Christians neglect. What happens in these times is often supernatural. God speaks to and through us as we pray for and with each other; and the obvious synergy gives a sense of the presence of God that one rarely experiences alone. I believe this is what Jesus meant when he promised, *"For where **two or** *three* **are gathered** together in My name, I am there in the midst of them (Matt. 18:20)."*

Many new Christians worry, not just "how" to pray, but "how often." In one sense, we are praying all the time. If we're aware of God's presence and silently talking to him in our minds throughout the day, we are praying "without ceasing" (I Thess 5:17). Having said this, it's also good to have one or two more formal times where we get on our knees, or if we're unable to kneel, sit quietly and talk to God.

I think it's also important here to remember that musical prayer is also critical to our growth. The book of Psalms contains actual lyrics of songs used to praise God. My wife and I often find that listening to praise music when praying helps us connect with God. Of course, the collective singing of prayers or praises in church services is just another kind of prayer—but an important one nonetheless.

There are many good books on prayer including Jim Cymbala's best-seller, "Fresh Wind, Fresh Fire." If you'd like help learning more or figuring-out the best way to build your prayer life, please email or call us at office@lifewaych.com or (860) 436-9216.

Before we leave the subject of prayer, I want to mention an advanced discipline that often accompanies prayer, especially when you feel "stuck" spiritually or are facing an exceptionally difficult trial. Fasting, going without food for a day or more, can create a deeper reliance on God and jump start your prayer life. Campus Crusade for Christ has some excellent material on how to fast effectively. Visit them at www.cru.org and type "fasting" in the search box on their main page.

Bible Study

I love the Bible. I know how bizarre that sounds in today's culture, but it's true. I believe that manuscript evidence, archeological evidence, historical analysis, and just plain old human reason shows that the Bible is God-breathed and without error as originally inspired and written.

What's not to love?

Therefore, since I believe God wrote it through 40 different men over about a 1,600 year time period, I love reading it because I believe God speaks to me and others through it. The hard part is that there are some sections which seem hard to understand and, with the wrong translation, might be down-right confusing!

So what I recommend is the following. These tips should help you get started. Once you're established in Bible reading and Bible study, books like "How to Read the Bible for All Its Worth," by Stuart and Fee will help you go deeper. But for now, try this:

1. Find an accurate, but easy-for-you-to-read translation. I think there are some wonderful options today which provide a great balance between readability and accuracy. Some examples are the English Standard Version (ESV), Holman Christian Standard Version (HCSV), New King James Version (NKJV), the New Living Translation (NLT), and the 1984 (nothing later) of the New International Version (NIV). Avoid paraphrases like the Message or the Living Bible. Frankly, you don't need them since these others are so easy to read and, they really aren't accurate such that they can lead to confusion. You might also benefit from the Life Application Study Bible or a similar Study Bible due to the helpful footnotes and background material included.

2. Try starting with the Gospel of John and reading 2-3 chapters a day. When you're done with John, go back to Matthew and read through all of the New Testament. Then, start in Genesis and do the same with the Old Testament. You'll actually read the Bible through in a year. See your church pastor or other leaders for help in understanding or finding good commentaries/study guides to help as you go.

3. Try praying before you read. Ask God to show you how each passage relates to you. Look for a major theme in each chapter, thoughts that support the theme, and the main thrust or call to action in that chapter as well. Consider writing a journal where you record what you hear God speaking to you as you read and study.

4. Join a good Bible Study group at your church. Studying the Bible with others adds insight and can also help you avoid misinterpretation.

There's a lot more which could be said on this subject, but the key here is to get you started. If we can be of help going beyond this point, please contact us—we'd love to help!

Service

As human beings living in a "me-oriented" culture, our natural inclination is to "take care of number one." I've even heard sermons where pastors tell people, "Well you know, you can't help someone else if you don't take care of yourself first." And, while there is some truth to that, the Bible seems to assume that we all take care of ourselves automatically, but must LEARN to serve or take care of others (See Eph. 5:28-29 for example).

The fear we have in this is that if we serve others, we'll lose or be taken advantage of. We're afraid that if we sacrifice our time and effort, there will be less left over for us to enjoy.

Several years ago, I was leading the youth group at our local church as a volunteer. We had an active Christian sports program, bible studies, meetings, practices, and more. One day, one of the deacons stopped me in the hallway and said, "Don't you worry that they (the Pastor and others) are taking advantage of you?" I thought about it for a minute and said, "Well, I hope so. I WANT them to take advantage of my gifts and training don't I?" He looked baffled as I walked away.

Looking back, I have to say that for once, I was right. My whole career has been based on people taking advantage of the gifts I have and I have had opportunities to travel, speak, train, and influence the lives of thousands of people. This has been more fulfilling and joy-producing than anything I could have planned or imagined for my life. Service has not been a loss-producing sacrifice. Rather, it has produced blessing…time and time again!

So trust God. Serve and trust that He will take care of your needs. Trust that IN the service, you'll find self-actualization and joy.

But first, you must find where to serve. I believe that we all should focus on the things we do best—the things God created us to do. How do you know what those are? My book, "Whole 4 Life" may be helpful in understanding what makes you unique.[4] I also have found Rick Warren's S.H.A.P.E profile to be of value. We use it in our church or you can find it via. Saddleback Ministries or Rick's book, "Purpose Driven Life."[5]. S.H.A.P.E. stands for Spiritual Gifts, Heart, Abilities, Personality, and life Experiences. Looking at these, you can often find where you're best designed/shaped to serve.

Having said this, finding a ministry or starting one is often a matter of "trial and error." It's by experiencing different areas of service that we fine-tune our skills and become clear on where we "fit." Wherever that is—serve. You'll be glad you did!

Giving

Jesus taught us to, *"Give, and it will be given to you: good measure, pressed down, shaken together, and running over will be put into your bosom. For with the same measure that you use, it will be measured back to you (Luke 6:38)."*

Now as I often tell people, we can't say we trust Jesus by faith and then doubt this promise. He's either a personification of truth (John 14:6) or He's a liar. If He's telling the truth, then I can't out-give Him nor will I be "left in the lurch" by tithing or giving even more than that.

Notice something else Jesus said in Matthew 23:23--
23 "What sorrow awaits you teachers of religious law and you Pharisees. Hypocrites! For you are careful to tithe even the tiniest income from your herb gardens,[a] but you ignore the more important aspects of the law—justice, mercy, and faith. You should tithe, yes, but do not neglect the more important things."

"Tithing?" you ask, "What in the world is that?" Well actually, the word means "a tenth." It's the practice of giving at least 10% of your gross income to your church. "WHAT? T-t-t-t-t-ten—TEN PERCENT?" (I know you need a deep breath, so take one…you're going to be OK…I promise).

From cover-to-cover, the Bible encourages, yes at times even commands, that believers give a minimum of 10% back to God. But, as always, He promises to take care of us and give us even more in return. Sometimes, that's a monetary return. Other times, it comes in an even more valuable form. And, while we DON'T teaching tithing as an Old Testament law enforced on New Testament Christians, it is a new testament principle which is part of the overarching, eternal law of God. In fact it existed even before the Old Testament law was given.

You see, to God, money is nothing. And, He knows when we have it, we'll likely waste it. Even if we don't, the fruits of His Spirit, (love, joy, peace, patience, kindness, goodness, faithfulness, gentleness, and self-control), last for eternity and really can't be lost or misspent. Still, there are times when He blesses in physical ways as well. What's for sure is that if we give generously, He blesses even more generously (See Malachi 3:8-10 and Matt. 6:33).

In our church, we teach that tithing is just a starting point. Actually, many of our leaders give more than 10%. I do. I say that not to brag, but to encourage. You see, selfishly, I give knowing that it's the key to even more blessing in my life and my family's life. The root of that conviction goes back nearly 30 years.

When my wife and I were first married, we mistakenly believed that we needed to do what ancient Israel did. We didn't understand the difference between the Old Covenant and the New. So, as we entered our third year of marriage, we committed to give 30% of our income to God. As with Israel, 10% was for the church/ministry, 10% for celebrations and conferences, and a final 10% was for the poor, something we thought we'd have to do every 3rd and 6th year in a 7-year cycle.

I remember we lived in a run-down, one-bedroom flat in Lumberton, NJ. The floor was so warped that if you dropped an apple in the kitchen, it would roll all the way through the living room area and hit the wall on the opposite end of the apartment. The walls were so thin we could hear the neighbors fight every Friday night…and then we'd cover our ears so we wouldn't hear them "make-up" after the fight.

We were poor. And, Karen wanted to get pregnant and quit work to have our first child. We could barely make it as it was and now, we were about to give 30% of our gross income away! My hands shook as we got on our knees, wrote the first check out to the church and prayed over it.

Now, what I'm about to tell you is not normative. That is, I don't believe or teach that it will happen this way for everyone. I do believe God blesses. I do believe He provides for our basic needs. What He did with us though was proof that He is sometimes financially generous to an amazing, breathtaking degree!

Over the next 12 months I want from barely surviving to making over $100,000 per year. And this was the early 1980's. I bought a new car for cash. We bought our first home. We paid the funeral expenses for the mother of a friend who was broke. And, best of all, we were blessed with a baby boy, our son David.

You can't out-give God—but its sure fun to try! So go for it—don't be afraid. Trust the one who loves you more than you could ever love yourself!

Faith-Sharing

In Acts 1:8, Jesus told all of his disciples that they were to be His "witnesses." A witness is one who has seen or experienced something and can report it to others to demonstrate or clarify what is true. If you've come to know Jesus, you too are His witness. So who are you sharing that with?

I know it's scary to share your faith in our world today. You risk ridicule, rejection, even legal action in some cases. But, put another way, if you discovered the cure for cancer, would you sit on it just because some might not believe you? Never! And in knowing Christ, you have something—some-one—even more valuable.

So, based on the many commands and encouragements in the New Testament, we know we SHOULD share, but HOW?

I don't think it's as complicated as we sometimes make it. Your story of "walking to" Jesus is personal and nobody knows it better than you. Interestingly, there are people in the world who will relate to your story better than they would mine or anyone else's for that matter. So by just sharing your journey, some will come to know Jesus. It's that simple.

Now of course, you can and should invite them to your church and to meet your pastor, etc. Still, it's you they know and trust. If you use the first few chapters of this book to study with them and help them, you'll have everything you need to assist them in crossing the bridge of faith.

A few cautions however:

- Don't push them. Fruit falls off the tree when it's ripe. It doesn't need to be yanked.

- If they ask a question and you don't know the answer, don't freak-out. Just admit that you don't know and help them find the answer. That's a win-win proposition. You learn and they do too.

- Stick to the basics and don't argue the twigs and little branches on the tree of faith. Remember the essentials are what matter. Things mentioned in this book for example, not the timing of the second coming of Jesus, tongues, the rapture, or any number of other topics.

- Remember, the best evangelistic approach is relational and servant-oriented. It takes time for people to come to faith. The vacuum-cleaner-salesman-approach of some "evangelists" where they meet someone and try to talk them into "prayin the Sinner's Prayer" in less than 3 minutes, is often offensive and ineffective. Get to know the person and guide patiently as God leads.

- Remember as well that the gospel is deeper and richer than a 30-second sound bite. Everything Jesus is, taught, died for, rose for, is doing now, and what He will do when he returns –all of it—is part of the gospel or good news. Thus, again, take time to teach and share and learn together.

One final thought. A lot has been preached and written over the years about our reward in heaven. Some say it's gold. Some say a crown. Others have their own ideas—like whether or not we'll oversee our own solar systems in the re-created universe/"New Heavens."

But I'm a simple guy. I think the reward will be what God values most since He's the one giving out the rewards. I think the reward is people. People we'll spend eternity with. People who will say to us, "Hey—remember that time you talked to me about Jesus? Well, I listened. And I'm here now because of you. Thank you, thank you, thank you brother! I'm so thankful!!!"

What reward could be better than that?

Mentoring

As I mentioned earlier, mentoring is a lost art and forgotten discipline in much of the modern church (See "Finding a Mentor," Chapter 6). Part of this stems from the fear we have of "messing-up" when talking to other people about God.

We need not fear. I have learned that God can even cause my mess-ups to be "wins" for His Kingdom. Sometimes, even when I give the wrong answer, people hear the right answer. I'm serious. God still performs miracles of hearing, just like He did in the 1st Century (See Acts Chapter 2).

So the key to being a mentor isn't perfection or having all the right answers. The key is loving God and the other person enough to "do life" together once a week or so to share what you've learned, listen to what they're learning, read the Bible a bit and pray. That's it really. And the results will bless both of you.

Maybe you could read a chapter of this book together or read it separately and then just come together and talk about what you read. How hard is that? Back in the days of video tapes, recorded Bible Studies were the "latest rage." We used to say, "If you can operate a VCR, then you too can be a star!" Corny, I know. But we said it. But now, you don't even need the VCR—just take this book and go!

You see, I agree with an old Promise Keepers adage I remember from a conference I attended years ago. Everyone needs a Paul, a Barnabas, and a Timothy in their life. Paul was a leader/mentor who trained other leaders. Barnabas was a friend or encourager to helped Paul and others to "keep going" when times were tough. Timothy was a learner—a young leader who Paul built into as an apprentice. Mentoring helps us find and fulfill these roles.

So who's your Paul, Barnabas, and Timothy in the faith? Pray and find them, then trust God to use those relationships in powerful ways. Find someone who will mentor you. Find someone as a friend or coach. Finally, find someone you can mentor or build into using God's Word as the Holy Spirit leads!

Conclusion

As brief and simple as it is, we pray this book has been a blessing. We believe it can be a launching pad for deeper study on every topic we've discussed. Still, in the midst of your study, never forget the basics and the simplicity that is Christ. Walking the walk is the key. We KNOW, and history proves, that if you do the basic things we've outlined here—if you live out the "Magnificent 7"—you will be a mature Christian with all the blessings and fruit to prove it.

Here at LifeWay, we also recommend you take part in our ongoing "Growth Track" series of classes normally offered Sunday after worship services. Commonly called Class 101-401, these will help you apply what you've been learning in this book. You can contact our office at 860-436-9216 or email charity@lifewaych.com for more information on "Growth Track." Finally, we'd recommend you visit our Welcome Center and get a free copy of the book, "The New Believer's Handbook." This study guide will give you even more helpful information to assist you on your journey of faith.

Footnotes

1. Stein, Ben, "Expelled. No Intelligence Allowed," Video/Movie Documentary, 2008.

2. McDowell and Strobel, McDowell Josh, "Evidence that Demands a Verdict," T. Nelson, 1999; &. Strobel, Lee, "The Case for Christ.," Zondervan, 1998.

3. Rissinger, Joel L, *The Crucified Church,* (Newington, CT, Xulon Elite, 2010).

4. Rissinger, Joel L., *Whole 4 Life,* Newington, CT, Communicate to Lead Publishing, 2015.

5. Warren, Rick, "Purpose Driven Life," Zondervan, 2002.

Appendix

LifeWay Church Statement of Faith

1. The Word of God

We believe that the Bible is the Word of God, fully inspired and without error in the original manuscripts, written under the inspiration of the Holy Spirit, and that it has supreme authority in all matters of faith and conduct.

2. The Trinity

We believe that there is one living and true God, eternally existing in three persons, that these are equal in every divine perfection, and that they execute distinct but harmonious offices in the work of creation, providence and redemption.

3. God the Father

We believe in God, the Father, an infinite, personal spirit, perfect in holiness, wisdom, power and love. We believe that He concerns Himself mercifully in the affairs of each person, that He hears and answers prayer, and that He saves from sin and death all who come to Him through Jesus Christ.

4. Jesus Christ

We believe in Jesus Christ, God's only begotten Son, conceived by the Holy Spirit. We believe in His virgin birth, sinless life, miracles and teachings. We believe in His substitutionary atoning death, bodily resurrection, ascension into heaven, perpetual intercession for His people, and personal visible return to earth.

5. The Holy Spirit

We believe in the Holy Spirit who came forth from the Father and Son to convict the world of sin, righteousness, and judgment, and to regenerate, sanctify, and empower all who believe in Jesus Christ. We believe that the Holy Spirit indwells every believer in Christ, and that He is an abiding helper, teacher and guide.

6. Regeneration

We believe that all people are sinners by nature and by choice and are, therefore, under condemnation. We believe that those who repent of their sins and trust in Jesus Christ as Savior are regenerated by the Holy Spirit.

7. The Church

We believe in the universal church, a living spiritual body of which Christ is the head and all regenerated persons are members. We believe in the local church, consisting of a company of believers in Jesus Christ, baptized on a credible confession of faith, and associated for worship, work and fellowship. We believe that God has laid upon the members of the local church the primary task of giving the gospel of Jesus Christ to a lost world.

8. Christian Conduct

We believe that Christians should live for the glory of God and the well-being of others; that their conduct should be blameless before the world; that they should be faithful stewards of their possessions; and that they should seek to realize for themselves and others the full stature of maturity in Christ.

9. The Ordinances

We believe that the Lord Jesus Christ has committed two ordinances to the local church: baptism and the Lord's Supper. We believe that Christian baptism is the immersion of a believer in water into the name of the triune God. We believe that the Lord's Supper was instituted by Christ for commemoration of His death. We believe that these two ordinances should be observed and administered until the return of the Lord Jesus Christ.

10. Religious Liberty

We believe that every human being has direct relations with God, and is responsible to God alone in all matters of faith; that each church is independent and must be free from interference by any ecclesiastical or political authority; that therefore Church and State must be kept separate as having different functions, each fulfilling its duties free from dictation or patronage of the other.

11. Church Cooperation

We believe that local churches can best promote the cause of Jesus Christ by cooperating with one another in a denominational organization. Such an organization, whether a regional or district conference, exists and functions by the will of the churches. Cooperation in a conference is voluntary and may be terminated at any time. Churches may likewise cooperate with interdenominational fellowships on a voluntary basis.

12. The Last Things

We believe in the personal and visible return of the Lord Jesus Christ to earth and the establishment of His kingdom. We believe in the resurrection of the body, the final judgment, the eternal felicity of the righteous, and the endless suffering of the wicked.

(Adapted from the Baptist General Conference/Converge USA)

Bridge Diagram

(Artwork by Simon Wainwright)

5 in 5

1. Coming to faith involves <u>Believe</u>. Acts 16:31, John 3:16, and 2 Peter 3:18.
2. Also, you <u>Accept</u> God's gift. Romans 3:23, 6:23, 10:9, 10:13 and Eph. 2:8.
3. Then, you <u>Switch</u> to His plan. Acts 2:38, Matt. 10:38, John 10:27, Luke 3:8.
4. Then, you <u>Express</u> your faith in prayer. Rom. 10:13 and Matt. 7:7.
5. Next, you're baptized and take communion Acts 2:38-41 & 8:26-38, Matthew 28:19-20.

7 in 7

1. Fellowship. Heb. 10:25, Acts 2:38-41 & 20:20.
2. Prayer and Fasting. Matthew 6:9-16, I Thess. 5:17, etc.
3. Study of the Bible. 2 Timothy 2:15 and 3:16. Ezra 7:10.
4. Service/Ministry to others. James 1:27 & Gal. 6:10.
5. Giving. Malachi 3:8-12, Matthew 23:23, Hebrews 7.
6. Faith Sharing. I Peter 3:15, Philemon 1:6, Acts 1:8, Acts 8:4.
7. Mentoring/Discipling. Hebrews 5:12, Galatians 6:1, Philippians 4:9, Deut. 11:18-19.

NOTE: *One topic is discussed per week, one-on-one or in a group of no more than three people.*

Made in the USA
Columbia, SC
31 August 2021

44008106R00037